Raspberry Pi 2

William Rowley

Table of content

Book Description

This book is about Raspberry Pi 2. It starts by explaining on what they, what they are used for and as well as their origin. The features of this device are discussed in detail, including the operating systems that it supports and the differences and improvements it made in comparison to the previous models. The accessories which are necessary for this device to function effectively are discussed. You are also guided on how to plug these accessories into the device. Once you have booted the device, you will be guided on how to login into the system including using the default username and password. After reading this book, you will know how to install the different operating systems such as Arch Linux and Raspbian into Raspberry Pi 2. You will also know how to access the Raspberry Pi 2 remotely using secure shell (SSH). Management of the device, including addition of users and assigning passwords to them has been discussed. The book has also explored how to turn the device into a file and media share server and how to install Bluetooth into the device for sharing files. Turning the device into a musicbox and a Retro game console have also been discussed. The book guides on how to enable online anonymity by use of TOR server.

The following topics are explored in detail:

Raspberry Pi 2 marked a great improvement from what we had in the previous models of Raspberry. This improvement is in terms of performance due an improvement in the processor speed and amount of storage. This explains why most people have greatly turned to use them in schools for teaching the basics of computer science, and particularly programming.

The device supports numerous operating systems compared to what we had in previous models, which could only support Linux kernel-based operating systems. For instance, this model of Raspberry supports windows 10. One should know how to manage it, including addition and deletion of users, and as well as accessing it remotely via the network using SSH. When used as a media and file server, the device usually draws very little power. When a Bluetooth dongle is connected to Raspberry Pi 2, it can be used to communicate with other devices, including sharing of files amongst them.

Chapter 1: Definition

Raspberry Pi 2 are single-board computers which are made to help in the teaching of basic computer science in schools. Most of the teaching emphasizes on computer programming. They were developed by the Raspberry Pi Foundation in the UK.

The manufacturing companies of Raspberry Pi 2 work under licensed manufacturing agreements to come up with several board configurations of these. The foundation has made Arch Linux ARM and Debian for download. Python has also been made the main programming language with these. Other programming languages which are supported include Perl, Java, Ruby, C++ and C. Raspberry Pi have shown a great usage in Britain and by the February 2015, over 5 million of them had been sold. Raspberry Pi 2 was introduced on early February 2015.

However, these are available in only one configuration, that is, model B. It has a RAM of 1GB and quad-core ARM Cortex-A7 CPU. The supported operating systems include RISC OS, Linux, Inferno, NetBSD, FreeBSD and Plan 9. In terms of performance, Raspberry Pi 2 is more powerful due to its advanced features. They are also able to connect to the network via a Wi-Fi adapter or a user-supplied Ethernet cable. The earlier models of Raspberry Pi supported only Linux-kernel based operating systems. However, windows 10 is supported on Raspberry Pi 2.

The quad-core processor has made it faster compared to the previous models. In the previous models, the chip for the RAM and the CPU were combined. However, with the doubling of the size of RAM to 1GB in Raspberry Pi 2, these have been made separate. Due to this, one can run several windows simultaneously and the performance will not be affected making the Pi act just like the normal PC.

Accessories Needed

Note that the Raspberry Pi 2 comes only with the board. You then need a power supply, hardware, keyboard, HDMI cable, mouse, microSD card with a minimum storage size of 8 GB and an Ethernet cable or a Wi-Fi adapter for you to get started. A 5-volt power supply is also needed.

Note that the more the number of ports that you use, the more power will be drawn, so be keen on this if you need to save on power. If all the ports are to be used, then a 2 Amp source will be needed. The keyboard and the mouse don't use any power from the Pi as they are powered by a battery. You can also use your PC to power the Pi via the USB port on the PC. However, this should be done when you are not using other components.

You should also consider purchasing a casing for your Pi. This will keep it safe and enhance is look. To connect to the internet, an Ethernet cable will be needed. A Wi-Fi dongle can also be used although this might need some extra work of downloading the necessary drivers.

For the case of the operating system to be installed, it will depend with what you need. However, Raspberry Pi2 supports Arch Linux, Raspbian, Pidora and Ubuntu Snappy Core. If you try different ones, it will be better because the experience will be different with each OS and then you will be able to choose the OS of choice. Arch Linux has shown much simplicity to install on Raspberry Pi 2.

How to plug in the Raspberry Pi 2

Before you can plug anything into the device, make sure that all the devices mentioned above are all assembled. Follow the following procedure:

Fix the SD card into the SD card slot in the raspberry Pi 2. This will only fit in one way.
Identify the USB slots on the Raspberry Pi 2 and plug in the mouse and the keyboard into them.
Turn on the TV or monitor and choose the right input for it. This can be DVI, HDMI 1 and others.
Connect the Monitor or TV and the Raspberry Pi 2 using the HDMI cable.
You might also need to connect your Raspberry Pi 2 to the internet. To do this, use an Ethernet cable to connect it via the Ethernet port next to the USB slots. If you don't need to connect to the internet, you can skip this step.

When you are ready, that is, you have plugged in all the cables and the SD card, you can plug in the micro USB power cable. Once you have done this, your Raspberry Pi 2 will boot.

If this marks the first use of the NOOBS SD card and the Raspberry Pi 2, you must select the operating system to be used and then configure it.

How to Login

Now that the Raspberry Pi 2 has completely booted, you need to login and perform your intended purpose. You will see a login prompt once the booting process is over. To ensure security, you will not see what you type on the login screen. This is a feature in Linux for ensuring that the security has been improved. You can login using the default username and password, whereby the default username is pi and the default password is raspberry.

Once you are logged in, you will see a command line prompt which looks as follows:

pi@raspberrypi~$

Note that the above will only after a successful login, otherwise it won't.

You might not be interested in using the command line. This calls for the need to load the graphical user interface. Do this by typing in the command startx and then press the enter key on the keyboard. The GUI will definitely be loaded.

Installing Arch Linux on Raspberry Pi 2

Start by plugin in the microSD card into the PC. Find the device node of the USB drive by running the lsblk command. You can then partition the sd card using the fdisk command as shown below:

fdisk /dev/devK

In my case, devK is the node of the device. If you use the wrong device node, you may end up formatting your hard drive, so do this with much keen. The above command will open the fdisk prompt for you. If you need to see the available options, type help and then press the enter key. In our case, we need to format the sd card. Do this by typing "o" and then pressing the enter key. The old partitions will be deleted.

You can then type "p", which is for partitioning. To create a new partition, type "n" and then press the enter key. To make the partition the primary one, type "p". Type "1" to indicate that it is the first partition. After hitting enter, choose the default first sector. For last sector, type "+100". The partition should then be set to use the FAT 32 file system. Do this by typing "t" followed by "c".

The next thing is to create a partition for the Arch file system. To do this, type "n" for new partition. This should be followed by "p" to make it the primary partition and then "2" so as to make it the second partition. You will then be done. You can then write these changes by typing "w" and then exit the disk.

We should then download Arch files and then transfer to our sd card. Remember that we have created a FAT 32, so we should create a mount point for it as follows:

mkfs.vfat /dev/sdK1

You should be very careful with the device node. A boot directory should then be created as follows:

mkdir boot1

We have created a boot directory and name it boot1. The first partition should then be mounted as follows:

```
mount /dev/sdK1 boot1
```

The root directory for the Arch should then be created. To do this, we need to start by formatting the second partition on our sd card to use ext4 file system as follows:

```
mkfs.ext4 /dev/sdK2
```

You should then create the root directory as follows:

```
mkdir root1
```

You should then mount the second partition as follows:

```
mount /dev/sdK2 root1
```

The Arch Linux OS should then be put into the sd card. Login as the root user and then execute the following commands, one-by-one:

wget
http://archlinuxarm.org/os/ArchLinuxARM-rpi-2-latest.tar.gz
bsdtar -xpf ArchLinuxARM-rpi-2-latest.tar.gz -C root1
sync

The above files will be downloaded to the local file system. They need to be transferred to the sd card as follows:

mv root/boot1/* boot1

You should then unmount the partition and then unplug the sd card as follows:

umount boot1 root1

You can then unplug the sd card and start to use it on the Pi 2 having Arch Linux as the operating system. The default password is root. This can be changed by running the command passwd. You also need to install some packages since Arch comes with no DEs.

If you audio to be supported on your system, install the following packages:

pacman -S alsa-utils alsa-plugins alsa-lib alsa-firmware

Xorg drivers must be installed first before any DE can be installed. This can be done as follows:

pacman -S xf86-video-fbdev

Install mate on it as follows:

sudo pacman -S mate mate-extra

Note that Arch ARM contains the AUR repository which is already added into pacman.conf file. It is from this repository that you install packages.

Installing Raspbian

To install this, begin be visiting the Raspberry Pi site and then download the latest release of Raspbian from there. The download should then be unzipped as an img file. After this, find the device node by running the lsblk command.

In this case, let us the dd command so as to copy the files to the sd card:

sudo bs=4M dd if=/path_of_pi_image.img of=/dev/sdK

Once the process of copying the content into the sd card is done, unplug it from your PC and use it on your Pi. Note that the Pi contains no on/off switch so to turn it either on or off, just plug or unplug the power cable.

Once the Pi has booted into Raspbian, a window for the optimization of the OS for the device will be opened. You should expand the amount of space on the Pi to be used for data. The default system user on Raspbian is "Pi" and this can be changed. The default password can also be changed in the same way we did for Debian based system.

Raspbian comes installed with some packages. However, you can also install extra packages from the repository by running the apt-get command.

Rather than Debian and Raspbian, you can also choose to use Ubuntu Snappy Core on your Pi. Download it from the Raspberry Pi site. Once the download is over, you should use the dd command as we did while installing Raspbian. The command apt-get will not work with the Ubuntu Snappy Core, so don't try to run it. This is because it uses a different package management system.

"Vanilla" Ubuntu LTS can also be used. However, it should be optimized for use on Raspberry Pi 2. Download it from the Raspberry Pi site and install it on the sd card just in the same way we did for Raspbian. However, it is not supported by canonical since it is community developed.

However, Raspbian is highly recommended for use on Raspberry Pi 2. Many hardware will work out the box. The default DE on Raspbian is also easy to use due to its lightweight nature.

Chapter 2: Accessing Raspberry Pi 2 via SSH

To use GUI tools, then a keyboard and monitor will need to be hooked to the Pi for it to be used as a regular desktop. However, you can take advantage of the SSH (secure shell) to manage the Pi over a network if you need to use it headless. This helps in saving on space and making the hardware free. Before removing the keyboard and the monitor from the Pi, make sure that you know the IP address of the Pi by using the following command:

ifconfig

You will get the IP address of both the wireless Lan (wlan) and the eth0 (Lan card). This will depend on the connection that you are using. You should write the inet addr somewhere to avoid forgetting it.

Install both the openssh-server and openssh-client packages on the machine to be used to access the Pi 2. If you need to access the Pi via the network, use the following command:

ssh pi@IP-ADDRESS-OF-Pi>

The pi represents the username on the Pi. IP-ADDRESS-OF-Pi represents the IP address of the Pi which is the one we collected using the ifconfig command. You will be prompted to enter the password of the user pi. After this, you will then be logged into the Pi and ready to do anything to it. This can include upgrading the whole OS or installing extra packages onto it.

Chapter 3: Management of Raspberry Pi 2

You can add new users to the system and create home directories for them. This can be done using the command shown below:

sudo useradd -d /home/william -m william Exchange 'william' with your username.

We have started by creating the home directory for the user william which is /home/william. The next thing was creating the user and we have given him the name william.

For security purposes, we need to create a password for this user. This can be done using the command shown below:

sudo passwd william

To give the user william some super user do (sudo) powers, use the command shown below:

sudo adduser william sudo

It is good to note that all Debian commands will work on Raspbian.

Chapter 4: Using Raspberry Pi 2 as a Media and File Share Server

The raspberry Pi 2 can be used as a media and file server. You can then use your PC to do some other tasks rather than using it as a server. You will also notice that the Pi will draw very less power. The easiest way to convert your Pi into a server is to install the samba server. Install the following two packages into your Pi:

sudo apt-get update
sudo apt-get install samba-common samba

Notice that we have started by updating our system. We have then installed the two packages namely samba-common and samba. This should be followed by running the following command:

sudo smbpasswd - a pi

We are creating a password. We have used the use pi. However, if you had created a user, use that user name rather than pi. To tell on the available drives for the purpose of sharing, you need to edit the smb.conf file using the following command:

sudo nano /etc/samba/smb.conf

A section of each partition that need to be shared should then be created. Use the following pattern for this purpose:

[4TB] -> shared directory's name
path = /media/4tb/ -> shared directory's path
read only = No -> to make sure that it is not read only
browsable = yes -> make the subfolder of the
directory browsable
writeable = yes -> enable users to write to it remotely
using networked devices.
valid users = william -> the system user

Your Raspberry Pi2 will then be ready to be used as both a file and media server. Now the question is, how you play audio using the Pi. You just have to install Kodi which was previously called XBMC on your PC. You can then browse for the Pi's samba server from your PC. The

Chapter 5: Installing Bluetooth on Raspberry Pi 2

Bluetooth can be used as a way of communicating with the Pi 2 once it has been installed. You will also be able to use the Bluetooth keyboard that you may possess for your games console or tablet. Transfer of files from your laptop or phone and the ability to control the Pi 2 using the Wii controller will have been made easy.

The Pi 2 should have a spare USB port for the purpose of connecting the Bluetooth dongle. To check whether the Pi recognizes it, open the terminal and run the command lsusb. All the USB devices plugged into the Raspberry Pi 2 will be listed.

Note that the Pi 2 might see the dongle but is not able to do anything to it. Begin by updating the OS of the Raspberry Pi 2 using the following two commands:

```
sudo apt-get update
sudo apt-get upgrade
```

The software which does something with Bluetooth should then be installed. This can be done as follows:

```
sudo apt-get install bluetooth blueman bluez bluez-utils python-gobject python-gobject-2
```

The above command will install a Bluetooth GUI manager, BlueZ Tools and utilizes and Bluetooth support.

Although controlling Bluetooth via the GUI is much easy, it is also easy to control it via the command line. Again, to get into desktop mode, run the command startx. The Bluetooth manager can then be brought up by navigating from the star menu to:

Menu -> Preferences -> Bluetooth Devices

You then need to set the Bluetooth adapter of the Raspberry Pi 2. This can be done by navigating through:

Adaptor -> Preferences

You will then be able to give a name to your Pi for the Bluetooth network. You can also choose to make it visible by other devices or not. Set this to Always visible.

Your device then needs to be paired with another for communication purposes. They will then set up measures amongst themselves for the security purposes. Other devices also need to be made visible in the network.

The aim is to be able to share files between the Pi and the mobile phone. The phone's network connection should also be shared using Bluetooth. Turn on the phone's Bluetooth and make the device discoverable.

You then need to search for this phone from the Pi via Bluetooth. On the Pi, open the Bluetooth window and click on "Search". The available Bluetooth devices will be searched and listed. If your phone is found, it will be in the list. Right click on it and choose "Pair". You will then be prompted to enter a short pin code on both devices. This acts as a confirmation that you are in control of the devices.

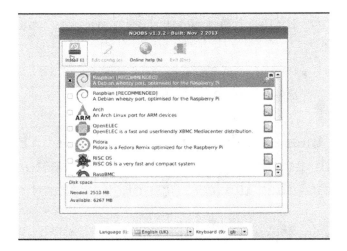

It will then be possible to send the files from the Pi 2 to the phone. Just select the file and click the "Send File" button.

Sometimes, you might not be having an access to a Wi-Fi network. You can use your phone as an access point. On the Bluetooth Manager, right click on the phone and choose setup.

Keyboard

A keyboard is a Bluetooth device. Just set the keyboard in pairing mode after setting up and starting Bluetooth on your Pi 2. Navigate to the Device Configuration window on the Pi and click on search.

After the keyboard has been listed in the available Bluetooth devices, right click on it and select pair. This is what we did with the phone. Follow the necessary procedure depending on your device. Some keyboards come with a default pin or there might be a pin to be entered on both the keyboard and the Pi 2.

Still on the Pi and on the Bluetooth Device Window, right click on the keyboard and choose Connect to Input Devices. The keyboard at this time should work correctly with the Pi 2.

However, note that once the Pi 2 restarts, the keyboard will not be reconnected. What you need is to avoid the process of entering the pin each time. Just go to the Bluetooth Device Window and right click on the keyboard Select Trust. You will have resolved the issue. The MAC address of the keyboard may also be needed. This can still be found on the same window, that is, Bluetooth Device window. Once you found this MAC address, you then need to add it the rc.local file as follows:

Begin by openi9ng the file rc.local as follows:

sudo nano /etc/rc.local

Add the following at the end of the file:

sudo hidd -i hci0 --connect MAC-ADDRESS

Where MAC-ADDRESS is the MAC address of the keyboard. This should be replaced by a number in your case. Make sure that your keyboard is on and then reboot your Pi 2. Your keyboard and the Pi should then work together.

Notice that in this book, we have given examples of keyboard and the phone as the Bluetooth devices to be used with Pi. However, the two are not the only Bluetooth devices for use with Pi.

The mouse and the Wii controller can also be used as Bluetooth devices. However, each has different instructions on how to connect them with the Pi. There also exist Python libraries which can assist you in controlling your programs via Bluetooth devices.

Chapter 6: Backup and Recovery of the SD Card

Backup and recovery of the SD card is a good idea and needs to be practiced from time to time. A second Raspberry Pi 2 OS on an SD card or a computer will be needed for this purpose. The type of computer you have will determine how the backup should be carried. However, an SD card or microSD card reader will be required in all cases. The type of operating system on your PC will also determine a lot. Let us examine how to perform this using different operating systems.

Using Windows

In windows, Win32 Disk Imager is a good tool for backing up and recovery of SD cards. It can be downloaded from SourceForge. Install after download. The next step is insertion of the SD card into the SD card reader on the PC and then start the software. A file explorer will be opened and it will show the contents or the files contained in the SD card.

Note that the contents shown will only be part of what is contained in the SD card. The contents which are not shown are not readable by windows. You should open the Win32 Disk Imager and use the blue icon to select the name and the location of the backup you need to take. The drive letter for the SD card also needs to be chosen. Once you click the "Read" button, the SD card will be backed to your PC.

Your card might become corrupted or unreadable during the process. However, just follow the above steps by selecting the image that you created as your image file and then clicking on write for it to be written back to the SD card. It is also possible to write it to another card of the same size and you will get an exact duplicate.

OSX

Begin by inserting your SD card into the SD card of your PC. Open the terminal. The next step is to search for the SD card. This can be done using the following command:

diskutil list

After hitting the Enter key, all the available disks will be listed. Search for your correct SD card. Be guided by the name and the size. If your card is /dev/disk2, you should find it in the list. You then have to create a disc image for your SD card. This should be in your home directory. Just open the terminal and run the following command:

sudo dd if=/dev/disk2 of=~/SDBackup.dmg

Wait until the command prompt reappears, meaning that the SD card will have been completely read. Note that the command will give no feedback.

Your SD card might also become corrupted or you might need to make a copy of it at any time. Just follow the approach shown above to restore so as to locate your SD card. Before writing to the SD card, unmount it first to prevent the operating system from writing it at the same time. Run the following command on the terminal:

diskutil unmountDisk /dev/disk2

To write the image back to the SD card, use the following command:

sudo dd
if=~/SDBackup.dmg of=/dev/disk2

You will notice when it finishes writing the image to the SD card. Just remove it from the Mac using the following command:

sudo diskutil eject /dev/rdisk2

Linux

It is good to identify the devices which are currently available before inserting the SD card into the PC running Linux. Just run the following command:

disk −h

The available devices will be displayed in a list. Insert the SD card into the SD card reader of your PC. Run the above command for the second time to establish whether the SD card is available. If you identify a device which was not present during the first run of the command, then it is the SD card.

You should then open up the terminal and then run the command necessary for backing up your SD card. This is the command:

sudo dd if=/dev/sdb of=~/SDBackup.img

Again, the dd command will not give you any feedback so wait until the command prompt reappears. This will be an indication that the process has completed.

For the purpose of restoring the image, just follow the above procedure to identify your SD card. The card also needs to be unmounted just as we did in MAC. However, the partition number should be used in this case. The unmount command will need to be executed for all the partitions on your device if they are multiple. The number of partitions is shown the df –h command.

The original image can then be written to the SD drive. The following command can be used:

sudo dd bs=4M if=~/SDBackup.img of=/dev/sdb

The option bs=4M has the purpose of setting the block size on the SD card to 4megabytes. In case of any warnings, adjust this to 1M. However, this will take a longer period of time to write. Wait for the process to complete before you can eject the SD card. You should be sure that the Linux system is through is through with the process of writing to the SD card. Use the following command:

sudo sync

Chapter 7: Raspberry Pi 2 Musicbox

The Raspberry Pi 2 can be turned into a real musicbox. This offers the following features:

Headless audio player. This can be played without the monitor and the music can be streamed from Spotify. Google Music, SoundCloud, Soma FM, Subsonic and Webradio.
Ability to be controlled remotely using a browser offering a very beautiful interface or using MPDroid for android.
Has DLNA and AirTunes streaming from your tablet or phone running either android or iOS.
Music files can be played from the network, SD card or USB.
You don't have to use the Linux command line, nor do you have to perform tinkering.
It supports Wi-Fi. Uses the WPA security protocol. This is achieved by use of supported Wi-Fi adapters.
Supports USB audio for all the available speakers, headphones and USB soundcards.
Supports HifiBerry which is a good Pi soundcard addon.

Requirements

SD-card
Raspberry Pi 2

Phone/computer or tablet for controlling the musicbox server
Amplifiers, speakers or headphones.

To setup the musicbox, follow the following procedure:

Begin by downloading the musicbox image.
Put the downloaded image in the SD card using Win32DiskImager.
Insert the SD card into the Pi and then boot it. The first run of the configuration will take 5 minutes.
Open the official musicbox web page and then configure the musicbox. The official web page for music is ww.musixbox.local

Chapter 8: Turning the Raspberry Pi 2 into a Retro Game Console

Compared to the first generation model, the Raspberry Pi 2 offers up to 6 times in terms of power. The cost is the same with the previous models and it takes no extra space. With this device, you can make a good retro gaming console. The software of choice in this chapter will boot direct into the emulator interface. It can also fit into the memory card of Raspberry Pi 2.

The Emulator Station is currently the best emulator station. It has been introduced into Pi as one of the RetroPie projects. It forms the front-end for many of go-retro game emulators. It can work on your TV visually rather than the monitor. The software is available for download on Emulation Station or RetroPie websites. RetroPie contains SD card images for both 1st and 2nd generations of Raspberry Pi. However, their compatibility is not 100%.

Download the software from the above sites and unzip it. Make sure that you download the right version. RetroPie is written and distributes as an img.gz file rather that the standard zip file. This compression standard is available for both Mac OS X and windows.

Making the retro brain

The needs is to prepare the SD card since we already have the image. In windows, this can be done with a lot of ease. However, we will discuss each and every detail associated with this. If you are not good in using SD card, begin by visiting the SD Association website and then downloading SD card formatter tool. There exist versions for both Mac OS X and windows.

It is a simple and beautiful graphic front-end. Just run it and then select "Overwrite" as the format type. This should be followed by selecting the name of your SD card. Retropie will then work for you.

The next thing is to burn the image into your SD card. In windows, visit SourForge website and download Win32 Disk Imager file. This will assist you in this. If you are using Mac OS X, download RPi-sd card builder v1.2 which is a Raspberry Pi writer software. If you don't find yourself comfortable working with this, download Pi Filler which is an alternative app for this purpose.

Note that off a graphical user interface so you won't go too far wrong in the process. It is also good to formally eject the card from your machine once the process of writing is over rather than just unplugging it. This will help in avoiding data corruption.

Booting up

Just insert the SD card into the Raspberry Pi 2 and boot it up. A rainbow screen followed by an Emulation Station boot screen. If you fail to see this, then know that you made an error somewhere. You can repeat the above process to solve this.

The next thing is to hold gaming ROMs. Note that the Retropie file system doesn't work just by dragging and dropping the files onto the microSD card.

Instead, use an Ethernet cable to connect the Raspberry Pi 2 to your router. The Pi 2 will be shown in the Windows Explorer section at the home section or on the finder of Mac OS X on your desktop or laptop. The ROMs and BIOS folders will also be seen in the file system. The ROMs folder contains sub-folders which represent every system supported by the Emulation Station.

You can reboot the Raspberry Pi 2. The Emulation Station Interface will show all of the relevant systems. Raspberry Pi 2 supports nearly every system including old systems such as NES, ZX Spectrum, C64 work and Intellivision. It supports up to systems of the 90s. However, at the end of 90s, this support stops. Nintendo 64, Xbox, PS2 and others are not supported. However, Gameboy Advance works very well although it is not a high power device.

How to operate the Emulation Station

Begin by plugin in the mouse and the keyboard. The software wizard will guide you to choose the keys to be used in the setup process. Controllers of many main consoles can also be used. Just try using DualShock 3 (PS2) by plugin it in. Use mini-USB cable. The Raspberry Pi2 will definitely see it. From the Emulation Station menu, you can then configure its inputs.

Xbox 360 controllers complicate the situation. Wireless pads are also compatible. The Raspberry Pi 2 should recognize a wireless Xbox 360 pad. To it should be attached a USB cable. Gamepads are also fully supported. Any plug-and-play pad should work.

In terms of speed, the actual emulation is great. Games such as Sega Mega Drive/Gensis will run at their full speed. The same case applies to all the SNES games. Super FX games such as Stunt Race Fix and Star Fox/Wing will show some visual glitches when they are run.

For the case of the trickier systems, the Emulation Station contains multiple emulators. There exist 2 MAME emulators, 2 N64 emulators and 3 SNES emulators available for the purpose of experimenting. T64 games will usually exhibit some kind of slowdown. However, not all of these games will run slow since some such as Mario Kart 64 exhibit a good speed. Some like Goldeneye 007's will always show an inconsistent frame rate and in open areas, it will take a real dip. Thus, it will require patience for you to play this game.

Some games such as The Legend of Zelda: Ocarina of Time can fail to work on some systems. The good thing with the Emulation Station is that it lets you to the correct resolution for your system. You can then choose a blurry or a more pixelated look.

Chapter 9: BitTorrent Sync- Bitsync

With bitsync, it will be possible to sync your files and folders across tablets, phones and computers. However, unlike what happens in Dropbox, your data here will be private.

Advantages of Bitsync

No third party access to your data as it is all in your hands.
The size of the data is limited to your hard drive. The size ranges between 1kb and 1TB.

Disadvantages of Bitsync

In case you have two devices and one of them is off, syncing will not occur. A good example is when you have 1 smartphone and 1 PC. If the PC is off, the smartphone will fail to sync due to this.

This explains the reason behind the use of Raspberry Pi 2. It also exhibits a low power consumption.

Requirements

You will need the following in this chapter:

A thumb drive (or a hard drive).

Raspberry Pi 2
Some type of display.
Micro USB charger
USB Keyboard
SD card
USB Mouse
Wi-Fi adaptor

Once you have assembled all the above, follow the following procedure:

Set up the Raspbian- start up your torrent client and then download the Raspbian image. Once the download is over, you should then write the image into your SD card. We have discussed this process in the above chapters, so I won't go about it again. If you don't know how to do it, just confirm from there.

Once you have burned the image, just plug the SD card into the Raspberry Pi 2 and then boot it. An initial configuration screen will appear. Just set your username and password, enable SSH, set the boot behavior and expand the root partition. Once you are through, just exit the configuration screen. You will then be on the desktop.

Install the BitTorrent Sync- connect the Ethernet cable to your Raspberry Pi 2 so as to be able to access the internet. Start the lxterminal. The next step is to download the binary for sync. Just run the following command:

wget http://btsync.s3-website-us-east-1.amazonaws.com/btsync_arm.tar.gz

Now, you have to change your directory to the download directory. Just run the following command:

cd /home/pi

Extract the download which is in tar,gz format:

tar -zxvf btsync_arm.tar.gz

The final thing is to run the program as follows:

. /btsync

We now want to ensure that the sync will run on starting up. This can be done as follows.

Change your directory to config folder:

cd ~/.config/

Create a new directory and name it "autostart"

mkdir autostart

Open the leafpad program and create a new text document. Add the following text to the text document:

[Desktop Entry]
Type=Application
Exec=/home/pi/btsync

The file should then be saved in the folder of the directory we have created above, that is, the autostart folder. Gove it the name "syncstart.desktop".

Once you have done all that, the sync will be running on your Raspberry Pi 2. To access the web GUI, you just need to open up the browser, and then type the following:

[IP ADDRESS]:8888/gui

If you don't know the IP address for your Raspberry Pi 2, just open the terminal and then run the command ifconfig.

At this point, you will be done and you can leave it as it is. If you need to have more space, just set up thumb drive. This is explained below.

How to add a thumb drive- it is possible to add space to the hard drive of your Raspberry Pi 2. To do this, just plug in an external drive. But in this chapter, we will use a micro-SD thumb drive. Open the terminal and run the following command:

df –h

Your thumb drive should be listed amongst the available devices. Just find it by name. Mine is named /dev/sdk1. Note the name of the thumb drive. The next thing is to format the hard drive. Achieve this by running the following command:

sudo umount /dev/sdk1
sudo mkfs.ext4 /dev/sdk1 -L SYNC

You might not be interested in setting up OwnCloud. If so, just leave at this point. However, make the sync to point to /media/SYNC. However, if you are interested in it, let us continue.

How to set up OwnCloud- this involves the use of multiple Linux commands. However, with Github user Petrockblog, this has been made very easy. You need to start by installing Github as follows:

```
sudo apt-get update
sudo apt-get install -y git dialog
```

Notice that we have started by updating the system and then we have installed the Github. You then need to download the setup script. Make sure you download the latest one as follows:

```
cd git clone
git://github.com/petrockblog/OwncloudPie.git
```

You then need to execute the script as follows:

```
cd OwncloudPie
chmod +x owncloudpie_setup.sh
sudo ./owncloudpie_setup.sh
```

The above commands will some time, so be patient. Once it is done, just navigate the directory [IP Address]/owncloud. Also, click on Advanced and choose /media/SYNC as the data folder.

How to combine OwnCloud and BitTorrent Sync-begin by clearing some of the file permissions. After this, add Sync to www-data-group. Just run the following command:

sudo usermod -a -G www-data sync

The sync should then write to the thumb drive. Use this command to enable this:

sudo chmod -R 770 /media/SYNC

Open BitTorrent WebUI, that is, IpAddress:8888/gui. You should then add a folder. Note that the files /media/SYNC/USERNAME/files should be added where the "username" is equals to the one you chose during the process of setting up the OwnCloud. After generating the key, you will be done.

The key can be used on any computer that you want for the purpose of setting up a folder. After any files on any computer are added to that folder, they will be automatically synced to your Raspberry Pi 2. You will them view them on the OwnCloud Web Interface.

Making OwnCloud accessible from anywhere- we need to access the OwnCloud from everywhere, including using mobile phones. A static IP address is needed for this purpose. In case you have used a Wi-Fi dongle, it will work just after plugin it in. Open the terminal and run the following command:

sudo nano /etc/network/interfaces

A number of changes will be needed for you to get the static IP address. You have to change your IP address, net mask, gateway, PSK and SSID so that they are compatible with your network. Consider what I ended up having:

```
auto lo
iface lo inet loopback
iface eth0 inet static
   address 192.168.160.30
gateway 192.168.160.2
netmask 255.255.255.0
auto wlan0
#allow-hotplug wlan0
iface wlan0 inet static
    address 192.168.160.20
    gateway 192.168.160.2
   netmask 255.255.255.0
wpa-ssid "Network SSID"
  wpa-psk "NETWORK PSK"
```

```
#wpa-roam
/etc/wpa_supplicant/wpa_supplicant.conf
iface default inet dhcp
```

For the OwnCloud to be accessible from outside networks, there is a need for the port to be forwarded.

Chapter 10: Raspberry Pi 2 Tor Server

Tor stands for The Onion Router. It is a system aimed at enabling online anonymity. The Tor client software has the purpose of concealing the usage or location of a user from anyone carrying out traffic analysis or network surveillance.

With Tor, one will find it to find internet activity such as online posts, visits to websites, instant messages and other forms of communication. It is good in ensuring the privacy, confidentiality and personal freedom while carrying out personal business to avoid being monitored. Due to these, benefits, a high number of servers are usually needed. Note that Tor is not a commercial organization. This means that many voluntary supporters will be needed. It is easy for you to turn your Raspberry Pi 2 into a Tor relay.

Requirements

The following tools are needed:

Raspberry Pi
network cable
power supply
SD card with Raspbian

Once you have assembled all the above, it will be time to start. However, don't work as a root at this time for security purposes.

Just do the following:

Open the terminal and run the following commands:

apt-get install sudo
        adduser tor1
            passwd tor1

You will have created a user named tor and assigned a password to him. The user should then be added to the sudoers file as follows:

Open the file /etc/sudoers:
            nano /etc/sudoers

Once the file is opened, add the following line to it:
            tor ALL=(ALL) ALL

Update and upgrade the system using the following commands:
sudo apt-get update
            sudo apt-get upgrade

The next step is configuration of the network interface. Just open the terminal and execute the ifconfig command. The present configuration will be shown. Note the inet addr and the mask somewhere.

The above should be followed by typing the following command:

sudo nano /etc/network/interfaces

The Raspberry will get an IP address from the DHCP server. In case you want to have a static IP address, alter this to the following:

iface eth0 inet static
address 192.168.160.22 <- Choose the correct one for your network. This applies to my network.
netmask 255.255.255.0 <- let it fit your network, this fits mine
gateway 192.168.160.2 <- this should be the IP address for your gateway.

The next step is to install and configure Tor. Just open the terminal and run the following command:

Sudo apt-get install tor

However, before running the above command, make sure that you are connected to the internet, otherwise, you will get an error. The download process will take some time so be patient.

The next thing is to edit the configuration file for TOR. This can be found in /etc/tor/torrc. Open it with the favorite text editor and perform some alterations to it. It should look as follows:

```
SocksPort 0
Log notice file /var/log/tor/notices.log
RunAsDaemon 1
ORPort 9001
DirPort 9030
ExitPolicy reject *:*
Nickname yyyy (choose the one you like)
RelayBandwidthRate 100 KB  # Throttle traffic to
100KB/s (800Kbps)
RelayBandwidthBurst 200 KB # But allow bursts up
to 200KB/s (1600Kbps)
```

The other has to do with the firewall. This can prevent other nodes from connecting to the TOR network, meaning that they will not contact The TOR relay. To solve this problem, the ports 9001 and 9030 must be opened. 9001 is for relay operation while 9030 is for directory service.

You are then ready to start the TOR server. Just open the terminal and run the following command:

sudo /etc/init.d/tor restart

TOR will then be restarted. Open the file /var/log/tor/log using the less command. Observe its end. If all is well, it should have the following:

"Oct 18 22:59:21.104 [notice] Tor has successfully opened a circuit. Looks like client functionality is working."

Conclusion

Raspberry Pi 2 are single-board computers developed to help in teaching of computer science in schools. Most of the teaching is emphasized on computer programming. The supported programming languages include, Java, Ruby, C, C++, Python and Perl. Raspberry Pi 2 was introduced early 2015 and it marked a greater improvement in Raspberry compared to the previous models. This is when compared in terms of memory and speed. Its memory for instance is of 1GB which is twice what we had in the previous models.

The device also has a quad-core processor which was not available in the previous models. There are accessories which are needed for this device to work, including the keyboard, mouse, monitor or TV and the cables and these have been discussed in this book. These accessories also need to be connected to the Raspberry Pi 2 in an orderly manner.

The device comes with a default username, which is pi and a default password, which is raspberry. You can use these to login for the first time, and you will be provided with a terminal. To get into the graphical user interface, one has to use the command startx.

To install the operating system on the device, the procedure to be involved depends on the kind of operating system, hence it is good to know how to install the various operating systems into the device. Note that the earlier models of the device supported only Linux kernel-based operating systems but the Raspberry Pi 2 supports even windows 10. It is also good to know how to write the images of the operating systems into the SD card. The device can be accessed remotely via the network using SSH. Files can be synced with other devices.